NOTE

Exam objectives are subject to change at any time without prior notice and at Oracle's sole discretion. Please visit Oracle's website (http://oracle.com/education/certification/objectives) for the most current listing of exam objectives.

SYBEX®

OCA/OCP:
Oracle9i DBA Fundamentals I
Study Guide